Contents

C.1

WOMEN'S PROFESSIONAL BASKETBALL

Teamwork:

The UTAH STARZZ

in Action

Thomas S. Owens
Diana Star Helmer

The Rosen Publishing Group's
PowerKids Press™
New York

To everyone who has waited or worked for a dream. Here's proof that dreams come true.

Published in 1999 by The Rosen Publishing Group, Inc.
29 East 21st Street, New York, NY 10010

First Edition

Book Design: Michael de Guzman

Photo Credits: pp. 4, 5, 19 © Nathaniel S. Butler/WNBA Enterprises, LLC; p. 7 © Susan Regan/AP Photo; pp. 8, 10, 17 © Norm Perdue/WNBA Enterprises, LLC; p. 11 © Noren Trotman/WNBA Enterprises, LLC; p. 13 © Bill Baptist/WNBA Enterprises, LLC; p. 15 © Norm Perdue, Bill Baptist, Noren Trotman/WNBA Enterprises, LLC; p. 16 © Rocky Widner/WNBA Enterprises, LLC; p. 20 © Nathaniel Butler, Tim O'Dell/WNBA Enterprises, LLC.

Owens, Tom, 1960-
    Teamwork: the Utah Starzz in action / by Thomas S. Owens and Diana Star Helmer.
        p.   cm. — (Women's professional basketball)
    Includes index.
    Summary: Briefly describes the first season of the team that lost the most games in the fledgling Women's National Basketball Association in 1996 and some of the talented women who play for this team.
    ISBN 0-8239-5244-4
    1. Utah Starzz (Basketball team)—Juvenile literature. [1. Utah Starzz (Basketball team)—History. 2. Basketball—History. 3. Women basketball players. 4. Basketball players.] I. Helmer, Diana Star, 1962-   . II. Title. III. Series.
    GV885.52.U8084 1998
    796.323'64'09792258—dc21   97-41101
                                                                                                       CIP
                                                                                                        AC

Manufactured in the United States of America

Shooting Starzz

The first season of the Women's National Basketball **Association** (uh-SOH-see-AY-shun), or WNBA, was almost over. The Utah Starzz had lost more games than the other teams. Now, on July 22, 1997, they were facing the New York Liberty—the team that had won the most games. The Starzz had played the Liberty twice before, and lost. In fact, no team had ever beaten the Liberty in New York. But this game was close. With only one minute left to play, the Starzz took the lead! They won the game 81 to 75!

◁ In this game, the Starzz worked together to beat the New York Liberty—one of the best teams in the WNBA.

5

Sisters to the NBA

The National Basketball Association (NBA), which is the men's basketball **league** (LEEG), started the WNBA. The WNBA idea began in 1996 when the Olympics were held in the United States. The whole world watched as the U.S. Women's Basketball Team won the gold medal. The American people wanted to be able to see these new basketball stars play in their own league in the United States.

The NBA decided that the women's teams would play in cities where the men's teams played. The WNBA would play while the NBA was on summer vacation.

Many players from the 1996 Olympic team, such as (left to right) Lisa Leslie, Carla McGhee, Katy Steding, and Sheryl Swoopes went on to play for teams in the WNBA. ▷

The Starzz Are Born

Fans in Salt Lake City, Utah, love **professional** (pro-FEH-shuh-nul) basketball. In 1970 the American Basketball Association (ABA) started a men's team there called the Utah Stars. Those Stars won the ABA **championship** (CHAM-pee-un-ship) their very first year! But five years later the team ran out of money and closed. Professional basketball returned with Utah's NBA team, the Utah Jazz, in 1979. The WNBA gave Utah its next professional basketball team, the Utah Starzz.

◁ The people of Utah were excited to have one of the first WNBA teams. And the Starzz have made them proud.

Most Valuable Player

Wendy Palmer was the Most **Valuable** (VAL-yoo-bul) Player, or MVP, for the Starzz. Wendy's coaches call her a great all-around player. She scores lots of points when she plays **offense** (AH-fents) and shoots. And when Wendy plays **defense** (DEE-fents), she keeps the other team from scoring. She gets about eight **rebounds** (REE-bowndz) per game. That's the second highest in the league!

10

Wendy Palmer is a great player, no matter where she is on the court. ▷

Elena Baranova

When the WNBA started, athletes from all over the world wanted to join. Elena Baranova came to the Starzz from Russia. Her team won the Olympic gold medal in 1992. She also played in the 1996 Olympics and for professional teams in Russia and Israel. Because Elena comes from Russia, she speaks Russian. Learning English has been hard for Elena. A **translator** (TRANZ-lay-ter) sits next to her on the bench for every game. This helps Elena understand her coach. And Elena is doing great on her new team. She blocked more shots than anyone else in the league during the first season!

Even though Elena doesn't speak English very well, she knows the language of basketball, and can ▶ understand her teammates on the court.

Playing for Fun

Tammy Reiss played basketball at the University of Virginia when she was a student. Coaches of college basketball teams around the country voted her one of America's best athletes in 1992. But America had no professional women's basketball teams for Tammy to join after college. Instead, she became the assistant coach of the University of Virginia team. When the WNBA started, Tammy quit coaching and joined the Starzz.

Tammy wears number 32 on her uniform. That's the number her hero, Earvin "Magic" Johnson, wore when he played in the NBA. "He played for the fun of it," she says. And that's just what Tammy does: she plays to have fun.

Tammy has always loved basketball. And even though she liked coaching, she wanted a shot at playing professional basketball. ▷

The Starzz and Their Fans

Playing wouldn't be much fun without cheering fans. The Starzz like to show everyone how important their fans are to them. The Starzz meet fans at basketball camps, stores, and at schools in Utah. Tammy Reiss once said that she answered all the fan mail she gets within a week. And that's a lot of mail!

Dena Head, another Starzz player, likes to talk to the people she meets. On an airplane, Dena once helped another passenger with her three children. The Starzz show that it doesn't just take a winning record to make a team of **champions** (CHAM-pee-unz).

The Starzz try to show young girls that they can do anything they want, such as play professional basketball!

17

Never Giving Up

By the last week of the season, the Starzz knew they wouldn't be going to the **play-offs** (PLAY-offs). They had not won enough games during the season. But the Starzz were happy with themselves anyway. They had beaten the number one team, the New York Liberty, in a game. This showed them that they were a good team and could win tough games. Throughout the season the Starzz never gave up. Their coach, Denise Taylor, said, "They could have quit, but they showed a lot of heart and effort. I'm really proud of them."

The Starzz always work their hardest and make Coach Taylor proud. ▷

Playing Together

Seven thousand fans came to each Utah Starzz game in Salt Lake City. Reporters say that Wendy Palmer and Elena Baranova will be seen as stars in the WNBA, especially as their team plays more games. The Starzz is the team with the youngest and most **inexperienced** (in-ek-SPEER-ee-unst) players. They may have lost a lot of games during the first season because they were learning how to play well together. This happens to a lot of new teams. "I think with every game we've played, we've grown up," Coach Taylor said.

◁ Wendy Palmer and Elena Baranova are two of Utah's stars.

21

Seeing More Starzz

Fans keep coming back to watch the Starzz. The people of Salt Lake City like that some of the players will stay and sign **autographs** (AW-tuh-grafs) after every home game. The players are friendly and excited to talk to their fans. After their last home game of the first season, Coach Taylor thanked the crowd. Then the players went into the stands and shook hands with fans! The Starzz love Utah, and Utah loves its Starzz. The fans are eager to watch their Starzz shine.

Web Sites:

To learn more about women's professional basketball, check out these Web sites:

http://www.wnba.com

http://www.fullcourt.com

Glossary

association (uh-SOH-see-AY-shun) A group of people who share an interest.

autograph (AW-tuh-graf) The signature of a famous person.

champion (CHAM-pee-un) A person or team that is the best in a sport.

championship (CHAM-pee-un-ship) The last game of the year between the two best teams in a league. The winner is the champion.

defense (DEE-fents) When a team tries to stop the other team from scoring in a game.

inexperienced (in-ek-SPEER-ee-unst) To be new at something.

league (LEEG) A group of teams that play against each other in the same sport.

offense (AH-fents) When a team tries to score points in a game.

play-off (PLAY-off) A game played at the end of a season to see which team is the best.

professional (pro-FEH-shuh-nul) When athletes are paid to play a sport.

rebound (REE-bownd) When one team misses a basket and the other team gets the basketball.

translator (TRANZ-lay-ter) A person who can listen to someone speak in one language and then tell someone else what the person said in a different language.

valuable (VAL-yoo-bul) To be very important.

23

Index

24